D1220695

My United States

Indiana

WITHDRAWN

T A M R A   B .   O R R

Children's Press®
An Imprint of Scholastic Inc.

11/18

J977.2
ORR

Content Consultant

James Wolfinger, PhD, Associate Dean and Professor
College of Education, DePaul University, Chicago, Illinois

Library of Congress Cataloging-in-Publication Data
Names: Orr, Tamra B., author.
Title: Indiana / by Tamra B. Orr.
Description: New York, NY : Children's Press, an imprint of Scholastic Inc., [2018] | Series: A true book |
    Includes bibliographical references and index.
Identifiers: LCCN 2017025785 | ISBN 9780531231647 (library binding) | ISBN   9780531247150 (pbk.)
    Subjects: LCSH: Indiana—Juvenile literature.
Classification: LCC F526.3 .O77 2018 | DDC 977.2—dc23
LC record available at https://lccn.loc.gov/2017025785

Photos ©: cover: Charles Cook/Getty Images; back cover bottom: russellkord.com/age fotostock; back cover ribbon: AliceLiddelle/Getty Images; 3 bottom: Dennis MacDonald/Alamy Images; 3 map: Jim McMahon; 4 left: Ellen McKnight/Alamy Images; 4 right: Foodio/Shutterstock; 5 bottom: Mikael Damkier/Shutterstock; 5 top: Sgoodwin4813/Dreamstime; 6 inset: Frank Jansky/ZUMA Press, Inc./Alamy Images; 7 top: Jared C. Tilton/Getty Images; 7 center: Wally McNamee/Corbis/Getty Images; 7 bottom: Daniel Dempster Photography/Alamy Images; 8-9: Pete Mcbride/Getty Images; 11: Bruce Dale/National Geographic/Getty Images; 12: PJF Military Collection/Alamy Images; 13: Arthur Smith III/Grant Heilman Photography, Inc.; 14 top: Steve Raymer/Getty Images; 14 inset: Frank Cezus/Getty Images; 15: Sean Crane/Minden Pictures/Getty Images; 16-17: Andre Jenny/The Image Works; 19: Chad Buchanan/Getty Images; 20: Tigatelu/Dreamstime; 22 left: Jamie Stead/age fotostock; 22 right: worldwideweberdesign/Getty Images; 23 top left: Alan Murphy/Minden Pictures/Superstock, Inc.; 23 bottom left: Ellen McKnight/Alamy Images; 23 center right: Atomic Imagery/Media Bakery; 23 center right: DNY59/Getty Images; 23 bottom right: Scott Camazine/Science Source; 23 top right: Foodio/Shutterstock; 24-25: Chase Studio/Science Source; 27: World History Archive/Topham/The Image Works; 29: Sarin Images/The Granger Collection; 30 top left: David & Micha Sheldon/Getty Images; 30 bottom: Popperfoto/Getty Images; 30 top right: Jamie Stead/age fotostock; 31 bottom right: Science History Images/Alamy Images; 31 top right: Matt Detrich/Getty Images; 31 top left: Jamie Squire/Getty Images; 31 bottom left: Margaret Bourke-White/The LIFE Picture Collection/Getty Images; 32: Margaret Bourke-White/The LIFE Picture Collection/Getty Images; 33: Paul Fearn/Alamy Images; 34-35: James Kirkikis/Shutterstock; 36: Jamie Squire/Getty Images; 37: Sgoodwin4813/Dreamstime; 38: Kevin Everest/AP Images; 39: Ty Wright/Bloomberg/Getty Images; 40 inset: Brian Hagiwara/Getty Images; 40 bottom: PepitoPhotos/iStockphoto; 41: wplynn/Flickr; 42 top left: John Paul Filo/CBS Photo Archive/Getty Images; 42 top right: Jonathan Kirn/Liaison/Getty Images; 42 bottom left: Granamour Weems Collection/Alamy Images; 42 bottom right: Mark Wilson/Getty Images; 43 top left: Kevin.Mazur/INACTIVE/Getty Images; 43 top right: Gilbert Carrasquillo/GC Images/Getty Images; 43 bottom left: Jeff Golden/Getty Images; 43 bottom right: Alexander Tamargo/Getty Images; 44 top left: FBI/Science Source; 44 bottom: Mikael Damkier/Shutterstock; 44 top right: 615 collection/Alamy Images; 45 center right: nimon/Shutterstock; 45 center left: Just Jefa/Flickr; 45 bottom: M. Unal Ozmen/Shutterstock; 45 top: Jim Hammer/EyeEm/Getty Images. Maps by Map Hero, Inc.

SCHOLASTIC, CHILDREN'S PRESS, A TRUE BOOK™, and associated logos are trademarks and/or registered trademarks of Scholastic Inc.

SCHOLASTIC INC., 557 BROADWAY, NEW YORK, NY 10012

1 2 3 4 5 6 7 8 9 10 R 27 26 25 24 23 22 21 20 19 18

Front cover: Lighthouse on Lake Michigan
Back cover: Sand dunes

Welcome to Indiana

Find the Truth!

Everything you are about to read is true *except* for one of the sentences on this page.

Which one is **TRUE**?

T or F The first Europeans to visit Indiana were Spanish explorers.

T or F Twenty thousand tons of ice cream are served each year at the Indiana State Fair.

Find the answers in this book.

Contents

Map: This Is Indiana! **6**

1 Land and Wildlife

What is the terrain of Indiana like
and what kinds of wildlife live there? **9**

2 Government

What are the different parts
of Indiana's government? **17**

THE BIG TRUTH!

Sugar
cream pie

What Represents Indiana?

Which designs, objects, plants, and
animals symbolize Indiana? **22**

Peony

Indiana State Fair

3 History

How did Indiana become the state it is today? . . . **25**

4 Culture

What do the people of Indiana do
for work and fun? **35**

Famous People **42**

Did You Know That **44**

Resources **46**

Important Words **47**

Index **48**

About the Author **48**

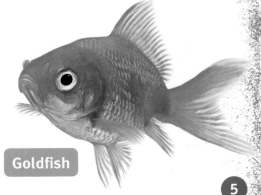

Goldfish

LAKE MICHIGAN

MICHIGAN

N W E S

University of Notre Dame

National New York Central Railroad Museum

SOUTH BEND

①

GARY

Indiana Dunes National Lakeshore

Hoosier Buggy Shop

Maumee

Kankakee

FORT WAYNE

Foellinger-Freimann Botanical Conservatory

Jasper-Pulaski State Fish and Wildlife Area

INDIANA

Quilters Hall of Fame

LAFAYETTE

Wabash

OHIO

ILLINOIS

MUNCIE

② Conner Prairie Interactive History Park

Ernie Pyle WWII Museum

INDIANAPOLIS

Indianapolis Motor Speedway

Indiana State Capitol

③

Eiteljorg Museum of American Indians and Western Art

TERRE HAUTE

Indiana University

0   30
Miles

BLOOMINGTON

West Fork White

East Fork White

George Rogers Clark National Historical Park

Marengo Cave National Landmark

Wabash

④

NEW ALBANY

Lincoln Boyhood National Memorial

EVANSVILLE

Wyandotte Caves State Recreation Area

Ohio

① University of Notre Dame

This university in South Bend is well known for its football team, the Fighting Irish. The school's famous golden dome is covered in real gold.

IRISH

6

This Is Indiana!

❷ Conner Prairie Interactive History Park

Step back in time when visiting this 800-acre (324-hectare) history park just outside Indianapolis. Find out what life was like for Indianans in the 1800s. Add to the adventure by crossing a 30-foot (9-meter) suspension bridge and walking into a 45-foot-tall (14-m) tree house.

❸ Indianapolis Motor Speedway

For more than a century, people have come from all over the world to watch the Indianapolis 500 at this racetrack. The track is 2.5 miles (4 kilometers) long, and drivers circle it 200 times during the race.

❹ Lincoln Boyhood National Memorial

President Abraham Lincoln spent his childhood in rural Indiana. Visit his boyhood home to learn more about his extraordinary life.

KENTU

A

Indiana is home to about 14,700,000 acres (5,948,879 ha.) of farmland.

CHAPTER 1

Land and Wildlife

Welcome to Indiana, a land of green rolling hills, flat **plains**, and thick forests. At just over 36,000 square miles (93,240 square kilometers), it is one of the country's smallest states. However, it has a great deal of excitement and beauty packed within its borders. It has everything from sandy dunes and deep blue lakes in the north to huge horse-plowed fields in Amish country and rich **limestone** deposits in the south.

Topographical Map

Indiana is divided into three regions, and all involve plains. The Great Lakes Plains region is covered in rich, **fertile** soil that is perfect for growing crops. This area has many small lakes and low hills created long ago by melting **glaciers**. The Till Plains region has rolling hills and valleys and is part of the famous Corn Belt. The Southern Hills and Lowlands area has steep hills and deep, winding caverns carved through limestone.

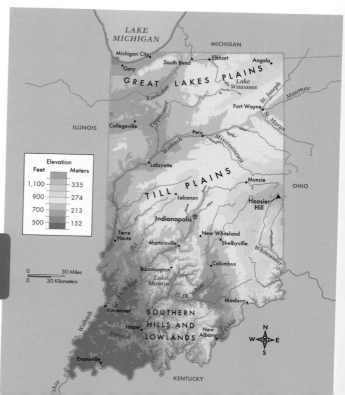

This map shows where the higher (orange and red) and lower (green) areas are in Indiana.

Elevation

Feet	Meters
1,100	335
900	274
700	213
500	152

0   30 Miles
0   30 Kilometers

LAKE MICHIGAN
MICHIGAN
Michigan City
South Bend • Elkhart
Gary
Angola
GREAT LAKES PLAINS
Lake Wawasee
Kankakee
St. Joseph
Maumee
Fort Wayne
St. Marys
ILLINOIS
Collegeville
Tippecanoe
Peru
Wabash
Mississinewa
Lafayette
Muncie
OHIO
TILL PLAINS
Lebanon
Hoosier Hill
Indianapolis
Terre Haute
Eel
Martinsville
New Whiteland
Shelbyville
Whitewater
Columbus
Bloomington
Lake Monroe
E. Fk. White
Madison
Vincennes
SOUTHERN HILLS AND LOWLANDS
Jasper
Patoka
New Albany
Ohio
Wabash
W. Fk. White
Evansville
Ohio
KENTUCKY

N
W   E
S

Heading for the Dunes

If you accidentally stumbled into the Indiana Dunes, which are located along the shore of Lake Michigan, you might worry that you were in the middle of a desert. The area is home to huge ridges and valleys made of sand. Some dunes are 200 feet (61 m) tall.

It's not a desert, though. The waves of Lake Michigan crash against the nearby shore, so there is plenty of water in the region. The Indiana Dunes stretch across 15,000 acres (6,070 ha). Many people visit in summertime to swim and get a suntan.

The Four Seasons

A common saying throughout Indiana is, "If you don't like the weather, just wait five minutes." The state definitely experiences a lot of different weather during its four seasons. Winter is often full of snow, especially for the counties closest to Lake Michigan. Summers in the state are hot and **humid**. High temperatures often bring powerful thunderstorms. Spring and fall bring pleasant temperatures, but tornadoes are common during these times.

Tornadoes can lift heavy objects such as school buses and send them flying through the air.

MAXIMUM TEMPERATURE
116°F

MINIMUM TEMPERATURE
-36°F

Indiana farmers use huge tractors to harvest corn and other crops.

More Than Just Corn

Looking out from Indiana's highest point, Hoosier Hill, you might get the idea that the state only grows corn. The state's Corn Belt is covered in millions of rows of green-leaved stalks rippling in the summer breeze. Farmers hope the plants will be "knee high by the Fourth of July." Indiana is also home to many wild plants. Flowers such as orange daylilies and bright black-eyed Susans grow along country roads, while birch, oak, hickory, and many other trees are found in the state's wooded areas.

At the Exotic Feline Rescue Center in Center Point, bobcats and other rare big cats are kept safe from hunters and other threats.

Indiana Wildlife

Indiana is home to many different creatures. Squirrels, chipmunks, and rabbits scamper across lawns. Raccoons and skunks visit at night. Deer walk cautiously through the forests. Rivers and lakes are full of catfish, trout, and bass. The air is full of song from robins, blackbirds, finches, and sparrows. A number of snakes slither along the ground, and more than a dozen species of turtles move slowly throughout the state.

Oriole

No Longer in Danger

In recent years, several formerly **endangered** creatures have made a great comeback in Indiana, including bald eagles and peregrine falcons. River otters, once a rare sight, are now found in almost all of the state's counties. Two decades ago, there were approximately 10 bobcats in Indiana. Today, there are more than a thousand spread out across 60 counties.

River otters relax on the ice at Muscatatuck National Wildlife Refuge.

Indiana's capital moved twice before settling in Indianapolis.

Government

It is easy to understand why Indiana is called "the crossroads of America." Several interstate highways run through the capital, Indianapolis, which is known to locals as "Indy." These roads can lead drivers to almost any part of the country. Indy is sometimes referred to as "Naptown." The name came during the early 1900s, when people paused in the city only long enough to sleep and then keep driving. Clearly, some decided to stay, since the city is now home to more than 850,000 people!

Three Branches

Indiana's government is divided into three branches. The legislative branch is in charge of making laws. It contains the General Assembly, which is made up of a Senate and a House of Representatives. Led by the governor, the executive branch carries out the laws. Finally, the judicial branch interprets the laws.

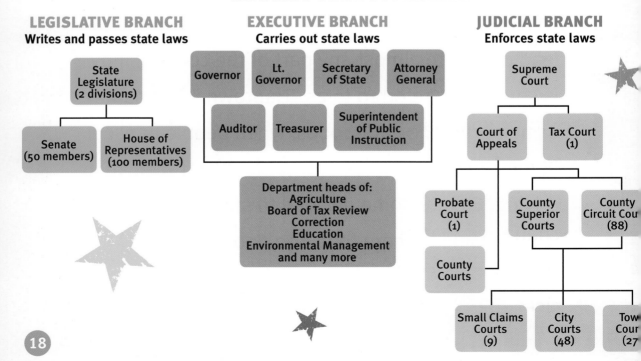

INDIANA'S STATE GOVERNMENT

LEGISLATIVE BRANCH
Writes and passes state laws

- State Legislature (2 divisions)
  - Senate (50 members)
  - House of Representatives (100 members)

EXECUTIVE BRANCH
Carries out state laws

- Governor
- Lt. Governor
- Secretary of State
- Attorney General
- Auditor
- Treasurer
- Superintendent of Public Instruction
- Department heads of: Agriculture, Board of Tax Review, Correction, Education, Environmental Management and many more

JUDICIAL BRANCH
Enforces state laws

- Supreme Court
  - Court of Appeals
  - Tax Court (1)
    - Probate Court (1)
      - County Courts
    - County Superior Courts
    - County Circuit Court (88)
      - Small Claims Courts (9)
      - City Courts (48)
      - Town Court (27)

State police are often tasked with protecting the governor and other state government officials.

A New Nickname

So far, the only Indianan to be elected president is Benjamin Harrison, who served from 1889 to 1893. However, Indiana has been home to six vice presidents: Schuyler Colfax, Thomas Hendricks, Charles Fairbanks, Thomas Marshall, Dan Quayle, and Mike Pence. This has earned the state the nickname Mother of Vice Presidents.

Indiana in the National Government

Each state elects officials to represent it in the U.S. Congress. Like every state, Indiana has two senators. The U.S. House of Representatives relies on a state's population to determine its numbers. Indiana has nine representatives in the House.

Every four years, states vote on the next U.S. president. Each state is granted a number of electoral votes based on its number of members in Congress. With two senators and nine representatives, Indiana has 11 electoral votes.

2 senators and 9 representatives

11 electoral votes

With eleven electoral votes, Indiana's voice in presidential elections is above average.

Representing Indiana

Elected officials in Indiana represent a population with a range of interests, lifestyles, and backgrounds.

Ethnicity (2016 estimates)

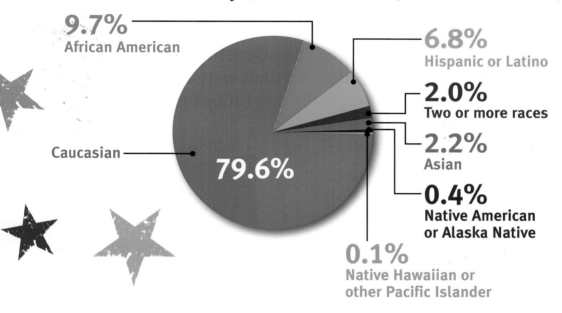

9.7%
African American

6.8%
Hispanic or Latino

2.0%
Two or more races

2.2%
Asian

0.4%
Native American
or Alaska Native

0.1%
Native Hawaiian or
other Pacific Islander

Caucasian

79.6%

24% have a college degree.

88% of the population graduated from high school.

69% own their own homes.

72% live in cities.

8% speak a language other than English at home.

What Represents Indiana?

States choose specific animals, plants, and objects to represent the values and characteristics of the land and its people. Find out why these symbols were chosen to represent Indiana or discover surprising curiosities about them.

Seal

The state seal displays an image of pioneer life in Indiana during the early 1800s. It shows a buffalo and a woodsman chopping down a tree as the sun shines above a green hill in the background.

Flag

Indiana's state flag was adopted in 1917. The torch represents liberty and enlightenment, while the rays indicate how far their influence can reach. The 19 stars surrounding it show that Indiana was the 19th state to join the Union.

Cardinal

STATE BIRD

This bird can be found in Indiana all year long.

Sugar Cream

STATE PIE

Amish settlers brought this sweet treat to Indiana in the 1800s.

Water

STATE BEVERAGE

This beverage was chosen as a symbol of Indiana's commitment to clean water and a healthy environment.

Tulip Tree

STATE TREE

This beautiful tree is also known as the yellow poplar.

Peony

STATE FLOWER

Each spring, this red and pink flower blooms in Indiana.

Salem Limestone

STATE STONE

Central and southern Indiana are home to this hard rock.

Indiana was once home to woolly mammoths and other huge creatures.

CHAPTER 3

History

Indiana's long and fascinating history stretches back thousands of years. From the earliest Native Americans to settle in the area to the state's newest residents, countless people have lived in Indiana. Each new group of people to come to Indiana has brought its own culture and lifestyle, influencing the way the state has grown and changed over the years.

The First Settlers

The first people to live in what would one day become Indiana arrived in the area around 10,000 BCE. They used stone tools and weapons. They cooked over open fires and slowly developed better, stronger weapons. Later, Mound Builders developed a culture in the area. These people created huge, earthen mounds for many reasons, from holding ceremonies and meetings to burying their dead.

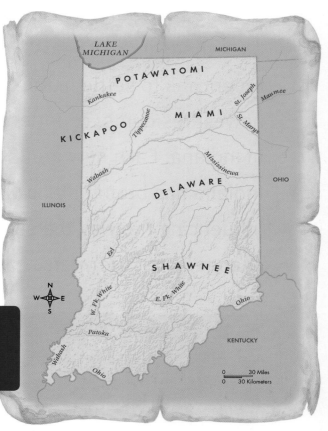

This map shows some of the major tribes that lived in what is now Indiana before Europeans came.

Over time, many Native American cultures developed in Indiana, including the Potawatomi, Kickapoo, Miami, Delaware, and Shawnee. Many of them lived in birchbark buildings called longhouses. These homes were long and narrow. They were often arranged in a circle. A protective fence or **palisade** was built around the circle. This helped protect the settlement's people from wild animals or threatening neighbors.

Visitors From Afar

European people first visited the land that would become Indiana in 1679. That year, French explorer René-Robert Cavelier, Sieur de La Salle, came to Indiana from Canada. La Salle claimed the land for France as part of a larger territory called Louisiana. Soon, more French settlers began moving to the region. At first, Native Americans welcomed the new arrivals as valuable trading partners. However, the French carried unfamiliar diseases that soon proved deadly to many native people.

This map shows the route La Salle took as he explored what is now Indiana.

Soldiers march through Indiana during the Revolutionary War in 1779.

The French and Indian War

During the 1700s, French settlers built a number of forts and trading posts throughout Indiana. Meanwhile, Great Britain had established a series of colonies along the East Coast. Looking to expand westward, the British went to war with the French in 1754. The area's Native American peoples also took sides in the conflict, which became known as the French and Indian War. France lost the war in 1763, and the land that would become Indiana fell under British control.

Fighting for Independence

During the Revolutionary War (1775–1783), the American colonies battled Great Britain to win independence. During the war, American forces captured several British forts in what are now Indiana and Illinois. This helped them secure the land between the Appalachian Mountains and the Mississippi River, and the area became a territory of the newly formed United States when the war ended in 1783.

Timeline of Indiana Events

1679
Europeans first visit the land that would become Indiana.

1775
The American Revolution begins.

1679 **1754** **1775** **1816**

1754
France and England go to war over the land that would later include Indiana.

December 11, 1816
Indiana becomes the 19th state.

The 19th State

In 1816, Indiana became the nation's 19th state. At the time, the capital was in Corydon, but it moved to Indianapolis in 1825. In the 1840s, Indiana's first railroad line was built, linking Indianapolis with Madison, Wisconsin. This made it easier for goods and people to reach the state. By the late 1850s, Indiana's population had passed a million, making it one of the most populated states in the country.

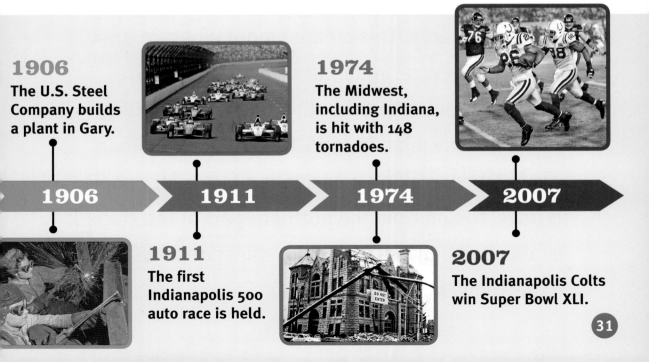

1906
The U.S. Steel Company builds a plant in Gary.

1974
The Midwest, including Indiana, is hit with 148 tornadoes.

1906 — **1911** — **1974** — **2007**

1911
The first Indianapolis 500 auto race is held.

2007
The Indianapolis Colts win Super Bowl XLI.

31

Many women worked in Indiana's steel factories during World War II (1939–1945).

As Indiana grew in size, more and more businesses came to the area. This created more jobs and drew millions of new residents to the state. In 1906, the U.S. Steel Company built a huge plant in Gary, bringing many jobs. In 1956, the Indiana Toll Road was finished, making it easier and faster for people to travel to and from the northern part of the state. It established Indiana as a major transportation route in the Midwest.

A Hero for Freedom: Levi Coffin

Levi Coffin (1798–1877) moved to Newport, Indiana, in 1826 with his family. Since his teenage years, Coffin had been an **abolitionist**. When he discovered his Indiana home was located along the route of the **Underground Railroad**, a network of locations where former slaves could hide as they escaped to the North, he knew it was his chance to get more involved. Using the wealth he had earned from his general store, he helped more than 3,000 runaway slaves find freedom. Coffin's home was called "the Grand Central Station of the Underground Railroad."

Dinosaur sculptures burst through the walls of the Indianapolis Children's Museum.

CHAPTER 4

Culture

Indiana offers plenty of things to do for both visitors and residents. Young children adore Indianapolis's huge Children's Museum where they can run, touch, and play. Older kids enjoy touring Conner Prairie to get a glimpse of Indiana's pioneer past. Families love the roar of the engines at the Indy 500 or the chance to go horseback riding or hike a canyon in Turkey Run State Park.

Big Fans

Hoosiers, as people from Indiana are known, love sports of all kinds. Basketball and football are extremely popular, and people often gather to cheer for the Indiana Pacers (basketball) and the Indianapolis Colts (football). They also follow college teams such as the Purdue Boilermakers and the Notre Dame Fighting Irish. Race fans flock to the Indy 500 every Memorial Day weekend to watch their favorite drivers.

Up to 350,000 people attend the Indianapolis 500 each year.

Ferris wheels and other exciting rides are part of the fun at the Indiana State Fair.

From Bridges to Ice Cream

Indiana has two very unique celebrations. In autumn, Parke County hosts the Covered Bridge Festival. The 10-day event has been held since 1957 and offers visitors tours of 31 covered bridges, live entertainment, and wagon rides. In summer, Indianapolis hosts the Indiana State Fair. The fair began in 1852 and has been called "Disneyland with cows and tractor parades." Twenty thousand tons of ice cream and 14,000 pounds (6,350 kilograms) of pork chops are eaten annually at the fair!

A research scientist in Warsaw works with a material used in knee surgeries.

Hoosier Industries

Indiana's people work in many different industries. One of the biggest is the auto industry. At factories across the state, Indianans help manufacture a variety of vehicles. Elkhart County is the center of the country's recreational vehicle (RV) industry. Other workers help manufacture medical devices, **pharmaceuticals**, and other lifesaving products. Agriculture and transportation have also been a big part of Indiana's economy for many years.

Changing Industries, Changing Jobs

According to state government reports, several areas of Indiana's economy will have tremendous growth by 2024. These include careers in the medical field, technology, and construction. Hoosiers—and future residents—will find plenty of jobs as biomedical engineers, psychologists, and physical therapists. Others will work as computer systems analysts, brick masons, and mechanics.

Time to Eat!

Indiana is known for its fresh corn on the cob. The state's people also enjoy corn dogs, elephant ears, peanut butter hamburgers, pickled vegetables of all kinds, and the king of sandwiches: the breaded pork tenderloin. This treat is often as large as the plate it is served on!

Green Bean Casserole

Ask an adult to help you!

This dish is found at almost every picnic, family reunion, and Fourth of July party in Indiana.

Ingredients
2 cans (14.5 ounces) French-style green beans, drained
1 can (10.75 ounces) condensed cream of mushroom soup
1/2 cup milk

1 can (2.8 ounces) French-fried onions

Directions
Preheat the oven to 350 degrees. In a mixing bowl, combine the green beans, soup, and milk. Place the mixture in a 1.5-quart casserole dish. Bake for 20 to 25 minutes. During the last 5 minutes of baking, top the casserole with the onions.

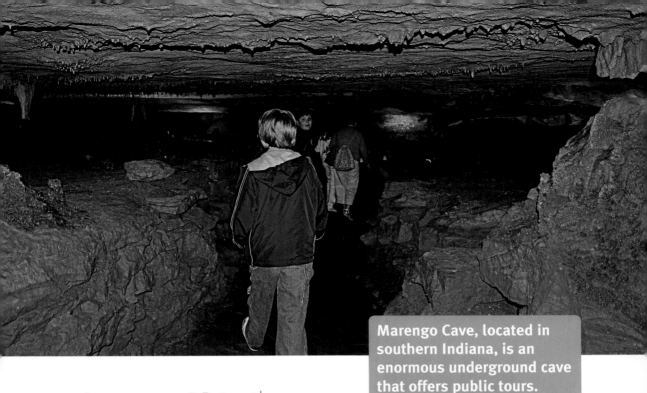

Marengo Cave, located in southern Indiana, is an enormous underground cave that offers public tours.

An Incredible State

Indiana is far more than just fields of corn and soybeans. It is a state that welcomes visitors, inviting them to sit down and watch the big game, munch on a local favorite food, or sit lakeside with a glass of iced tea in hand. Hoosiers are friendly people. They are eager to show off their state and let you know why it is one of the very best in the country. ★

Famous People

David Letterman

(1947–) is a comedian and former late night talk show host. Before he became famous, he was a weatherman for radio and television. He was born in Indianapolis.

Larry Bird

(1956–) was a professional basketball player for the Boston Celtics. Later, he was the head coach of the Indiana Pacers. Often called Larry Legend, he is considered one of the best players in NBA history. He was born in West Baden Springs.

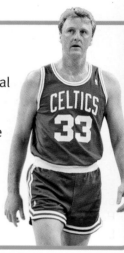

Mike Pence

(1959–) served as the 48th vice president of the United States. He was also previously a U.S. representative from Indiana and Indiana's governor. He was born in Columbus.

Michael Jackson

(1958–2009) was a singer, songwriter, and dancer who began his career singing alongside his brothers in the Jackson 5. Later, as a solo artist, he became known as the King of Pop. He was born in Gary.

Axl Rose

(1962–) is the lead vocalist of the rock band Guns N' Roses. Born William Bruce Rose Jr., he was inducted into the Rock and Roll Hall of Fame in 2012. He was born in Lafayette.

Vivica A. Fox

(1964–) is an actress and television producer who has starred in many movies. She was born in South Bend.

Jim Gaffigan

(1966–) is a television actor, writer, and comedian who has appeared in many shows and commercials. He grew up in La Porte.

John Green

(1977–) is the author of best-selling novels such as *The Fault in Our Stars*. He and his brother, Hank, are very popular on YouTube and have their own channel. Green was born in Indianapolis.

Did You Know That ...

WANTED

JOHN HERBERT DILLINGER

On June 23, 1934, HOMER S. CUMMINGS, Attorney General of the United States, under the authority vested in him by an Act of Congress approved June 6, 1934, offered a reward of

$10,000.00

for the capture of John Herbert Dillinger or a reward of

$5,000.00

for information leading to the arrest of John Herbert Dillinger.

DESCRIPTION

Age, 32 years; Height, 5 feet 7-1/8 inches; Weight, 153 pounds; Build, medium; Hair, medium chestnut; Eyes, grey; Complexion, medium; Occupation, machinist; Marks and scars, 1/2 inch scar back left hand, near middle upper lip, brown mole between eyebrows.

Angel Mounds is an archaeological site in Evansville. People lived there between the years 1000 and 1450. The site features 11 big dirt mounds that people used for ceremonies and burials.

Bullets from the John Dillinger gang, a notorious group of bank robbers, are still embedded in the walls of a motel in Indianapolis.

The first successful goldfish farm in the country was opened in 1899 in the city of Martinsville.

One of the biggest natural threats to Indiana is flooding. In 2008, the state was declared a disaster area due to flooding. In 2013, much of Fort Wayne was covered by floodwaters.

No one really knows why Indiana is called the Hoosier State. But over the years many stories have been told about its origins. One story says it comes from a Native American word for corn, *hoosa*. Another says it comes from "Who's here?," a question often called out by early settlers in answer to a knock on the door.

Almost 1,000 natural and artificial lakes can be found throughout Indiana. The largest lake is Lake Wawasee near Warsaw.

If you are under the age of 14 and live in Indianapolis, you can be fined $3 for every swear word you use.

Did you find the truth?

F The first Europeans to visit Indiana were Spanish explorers.

T Twenty thousand tons of ice cream are served each year at the Indiana State Fair.

Resources

Books

Nonfiction

Brezina, Corona. *Indiana: Past and Present*. New York: Rosen Central, 2010.

Ransom, Candace. *What's Great About Indiana?* Minneapolis: Lerner Publications, 2015.

Stille, Darlene. *Indiana*. New York: Children's Press, 2014.

Swanson, Angie. *Indiana*. North Mankato, MN: Capstone Press, 2017.

Fiction

Cabot, Meg. *Teen Idol*. New York: HarperCollins, 2004.

Green, John. *The Fault in Our Stars*. New York: Dutton Books, 2012.

Visit this Scholastic website for more information on Indiana:

★ www.factsfornow.scholastic.com
Enter the keyword **Indiana**

Important Words

abolitionist (ab-uh-LISH-uh-nist) a person who supported the end of slavery

endangered (en-DAYN-jurd) in danger of extinction

fertile (FUR-tuhl) good for growing crops

glaciers (GLAY-shurz) large masses of ice that move very slowly

humid (HYOO-mid) containing a high amount of water vapor in the air

limestone (LYME-stohn) a type of hard rock that is often used as a building material

palisade (PAL-uh-sayd) a protective wall or fence

pharmaceuticals (far-muh-SOO-tih-kuhlz) medications

plains (PLAYNZ) wide, mostly flat areas of land

Underground Railroad (UN-dur-grownd RAYL-rohd) a secret system used to transport escaped slaves to safety

Index

Page numbers in **bold** indicate illustrations.

abolitionists, 33
agriculture, **13**, 38
animals, **14**, **15**, **23**, 24–25

birds, **14**, **23**
bobcats, **14**, 15

capitol building, **16–17**
climate, **12**, **31**, **44**
Coffin, Levi, **33**
Conner Prairie, **7**, 35
corn, 10, **13**, 40, **45**
covered bridges, **37**

early settlers, **24**, 26, 44, 45
economy, 38, 39
education, 6, 21
elevation, **10**
endangered animals, **14**, 15
explorers, **28**, 30

famous people, **42–43**
festivals, 37
fish, 14, **44**
food, **23**, 40
French and Indian War, 29, **30**

Great Lakes Plains region, 10

Indiana Dunes, **11**
Indianapolis, **7**, **16–17**, **19**, 31, **34–35**, **36**, 37, 42, 43, 44, 45
Indianapolis 500, **7**, **31**, 36
Indianapolis Children's Museum, **34–35**

jobs, **32**, **38**, **39**

Lake Michigan, 11, 12
lakes, 10, 11, 12, 14, **45**
land, **8–9**, **10**, 11
languages, 21
limestone, 9, 10, **23**
Lincoln, Abraham, 7

manufacturing, **38**
maps, **6–7**, **10**, **26**, **28**
Marengo Cave, **41**
Mound Builders, 26, 44
Muscatatuck National Wildlife Refuge, **15**
music, **42**, **43**

national government, 19, 20, **42**
Native Americans, 21, **26**, **27**, 28, 29, 45

population, 20, 31

recipe, **40**
Revolutionary War, **29**, **30**
river otters, **15**

settlers, 23, 28, 29
slavery, 33
snakes, 14
Southern Plains region, 10
sports, **6**, 7, **31**, 36, **42**
state capital, 31
state fair, **37**
state government, 16–17, 18, **19**
statehood, 30, 31
symbols, **22–23**

Till Plains region, 10
timeline, **30–31**
tornadoes, **31**
transportation, 17, 31, 32, 38
trees, 13, **23**
turtles, 14

Underground Railroad, 33
University of Notre Dame, **6**, 36
U.S. Steel Company, **31**, **32**

wildflowers, 13, **23**

About the Author

Tamra Orr is the author of hundreds of books for readers of all ages. She was born in Elkhart, Indiana, and went to college at Ball State University in Muncie, getting her degree in English and secondary education. After graduating, she moved to Warsaw, Indiana. Now she lives in the Pacific Northwest. She is the mother of four children, and loves to spend her free time reading, writing, and going camping. She visits Indiana every few years to say hello to family and friends.